THE BLUE IN EVERYTHING copyright © 2020 by Samy Sharif Sabh

First Edition, February 2020
Blue Byron Books
Chicago, Illinois

bluebyronbooks.com

Editing: Joshua Bohnsack
Photos: Dan Kanvis
Production: Rich Hebron

THE BLUE IN EVERYTHING is under copyright protection. No part of this book may be used or reproduced in any manner whatsoever without written permission except in the case of brief quotations embodied in critical articles and reviews. Printed in the United States of America. All rights reserved.

ISBN (pbck) 978-1-7326882-4-7

ISBN (epub) 978-1-7326882-5-4

Dedicated to Mark Turcotte.
Thank you for the lightning.

Sunny/Sonny,

When I fell in love with your mother I will be in my thirties and everything will be good because each morning I'll wake up and write about you.

We'll talk about the blue in everything; posters of Hope and how they looked when they burned.

Sometimes things will be discordant because they'll make too much sense
    like asking Siri how to spell human obsolescence.
    Other times things will seem perfect and round
    because of jaggedness.

Your eyes will widen each year as the delicacy of this unruly madness reveals itself to you
    and it will become clear
    everything we know is rooted in pretending
    and that's what makes everything art; so here we are.

Words come from eyes;
eyes come from stars;
stars come from space;
space comes from time;
time comes from motion;
motion comes from speed and location;
and the more you know about speed
the less you know about location;
and the more you know about location
the less you know about speed.

                                          Love,

                                          Dad

OPEN ENDED LIKE 'U',

on the blue in everything

if you were Christ on the cross
if you were Muhammad and His holy Word
if you were the Virgin Mary and her
gleaming light
if you were a Saudi Prince that fell in love
with Rihanna
if you were Princess Diana's limo driver
if you were a virgin
if you were a suburban stepmother
with a husband
that definitely definitely definitely
doesn't fuck his interns
if you were the son of a diplomat
that moved from Istanbul–to
Cologne–to Marseille through your
good years whilst loving good girls
from good families with good salaries
and good morals
if you were a pilot flying over Hiroshima with a
general's order and a conscience you
never felt particularly tied to
if you were a president's daughter with
beautiful legs in magazines
if you were a sunflower that a poet found
if you were a school teacher that taught
cursive on monkey bars
if you were a templated inspirational Facebook quote
that you're sixth grade crush dropped like a dumbbell
on your shoes
if you were a street dog in Kathmandu choking

on your last crooked bone
if you were all the debt in the world
if you were a barfly with a coal miner's
lung for a liver
if you were a Tijuana whore covered
in blisters and mileage
if you were an aborted fetus that only
ever knew the truest silence of sleep
if you were truly your idea of yourself
you will have known the Blue in Everything
as well as the next sorry soul
that ended up on history's torn-out pages
filed in a cabinet
in an office
in a dive bar
on a quiet street
between
whatever flavor of Hell you prefer
and Neverland

every morning there's a jackhammer

…everyone all sunny yellow. men that are good with money. 401K boy wonders. women with the good teeth. women that like spanish wines. dogs; well-groomed and bright-eyed. i looked into the sun and now it's all i can see. little lens flares when i close my eyes…

sunny,

cell phones make it easy to get
from point A to point B and travel
makes you interesting at parties so you should do it
also some people say that not all wanderers
are lost so
walk in circles
in a forest or a desert
from time to time
because the story will be better

the way time speeds up with age

i've been thinking about sewing
my mouth shut
to lose weight
and get shredded like
fresh mulch
on my father's front lawn

rake leaves from
under a tree that
illuminates
the kind of truth
that alleviates headaches
and causes them
at the same time

i remove a dead shrub

see all at once

the hypocrisy of
being born

        sorting through
        selves like racks
        at a
        village discount

i want deeply
to be from the
pocket of God

and cut the part
of my head off
that lies
i want deeply
to be from the
pocket of God
and see wrinkles
like the insides of trees

and
do away with anything
that stands between myself
and the mechanisms i can't
see at work like
    the way time
    speeds up with age

sunny,

look for a ladder

someone to the left of me keeps coughing

take me somewhere dark and unschool me of these stupid tics. what's so wholehearted about a deflating balloon in a meadow? take me somewhere dark and unschool me of this cheap game. i masturbate too, man. it's ok. don't worry. the unschooling won't take that away from us. just the parts of our heads that lie and the dryness on our elbows. the center of a Venn diagram looks like a vagina. illuminati casserole. i'll love my brethren 'til the end. take me somewhere dark and unschool me of this impulse. i am an addict. i am an addict. i need sex and berries and nakedness and drugs both slow and fast. take me somewhere dark and unschool me. take me to a park and undress me. take me to your house and undo me. take me to Egypt and Ireland and show me the meaning of being a backstreet boy. take me somewhere where the truth burns like warm vodka. i am an addict. i am an addict. take me somewhere dark and unschool me.

some rules to live by

    1.   an ice cube is trained to melt

                                                        (no wait)

    1.   sex isn't something to put a frame around

                                                        (no wait)

    1.   heartache; it's only as meaningful as your reflection in a puddle

                                                        (yeah)

Prophet, please prophecy
What constitutes a lie
Prophet, please prophecy
What constitutes a life

sunny,

the reason i love sunflowers so much
is because you look just like one
and because I know you would never
turn your back on what feeds you
light

FISH HOOK
FISH HOOKED
FISH HOOKER

– THE BLUE IN EVERYTHING –

U,O.
SUN, SON.
SUNNY, SONNY.

templestowe

If you find something beautiful
beat it mercilessly until a poem falls out
and convince yourself that it's more
important than true self-actualization
until you're a lonely old bird
on a bar stool
where you'll
watch the news very loudly
so as to be sure you understand
that there is in fact
poison in the baby food
and you'll think back to another time
where you used to have sex with
killers and paralegals and waitresses
you'll ponder how
when you get older the things
that pierce your heart become different
and love becomes
less about resumé
and more about fresh produce
and good movies
and you'll realize that
if you drink late
into moon
into sun
enough times in a decade you can sometimes become
Bukowski and drink golden piss like the hopeless romantic
you are
and have become
through the art

of mediocre fucks tucked
between a pillow
and a mattress
where you would ask girls about middle names
and sometimes you'd sweat and labor
over the idea that you're all the man
you'll ever have to be
and you would feel many things
wretchedly profound and poetic
but you would not feel peace
and you'll deify cheap scotch
and you'll be thankful for
the lovers that made you feel pain
and made you fall in love with the way
that you feel pain
and that
you are most virtuous and present
when feeling pain
induced by someone
more comfortable
with the idea of a lonely night
and a clear head
and a glass of water
and a piece of fish
and you won't relate
because you love the way
the bar smells
and beating poems out of everything
beautiful until there's nothing left
but an old bird
on a bar stool

mistaking patterns for God, pt. I

in my parent's basement there's a photograph of a blue door. last night I slept there. there are two couches in the basement. one by the garage door, the other tucked in a far corner, closer to the stairs. my cousin slept on the one by the garage door. i slept on the one in the corner. the door to the garage is white. my mother says she wants a new front door. one made of glass to let more light into the house. we need more light in the house. my friend speaks Mandarin. he was just offered a job to sell private jets to Chinese people. i wasn't listening when he told my cousin and i about the offer. i was on twitter reading about Earl Sweatshirt. which is funny because earlier that day my cousin called me "chum." last night, on the couch in the corner, i had a dream. a really bad one. a nightmare. a night terror. i was on a plane. you were the pilot. my mother, father, brother, and cousin on board. you were flying the plane over the ocean, only you were flying far too low. so low the waves would graze the bottom of the plane. then a wave catches the nose. water fills the cabin. my family and i start choking but i see you escape through a window. I wake up. i see the photograph of the blue door. i fall back asleep. i dream that i'm in my parent's house with my mother, father, brother, cousin, and you circled around the breakfast table, only everyone's names are switched around. i wake back up and cry. i dry my eyes. i go upstairs to the breakfast table where my mother, father, brother, and cousin are gathered. you weren't there, though. my mother hands me a home appliance catalogue. "what do you think of this one, Sam?" she points to item C01863. it's a stained glass door. it's mostly blue.

fourth of july

there were times that I felt power in being
and all-American
while drooling over you in a Michigan town

you see
July is like you and you are like it
in that the great American holiday
is explosive and recollective

white denim and linen

strawberry stains

plain paper plate

still in my dreams like a
fever
like a
dove
like a
dead pigeon
like an
armed robber
       memory bank

kick me hard in the face with those hay-belted wedges

i like it

server farm // murder farm

hesitance isn't a polar wind

all my best ideas are   forgotten

    server farm
    improperly irrigated
    with regret

hesitance is an apple seed in hand

alone in a city
trying to dig through concrete
with your feet

a new
love that crowns
ambivalence as
certitude
and
certitude
as a tattoo at 18

    murder farm
    improperly tended
    with mercy

sunny,

when you're young
each day comes to you
with a piece of fruit
and when you're old
your job is to
remember the sweetness
so eat organic
and
remember things clearly

maybe if i turn the knife like this…

there's always a bottle
there's always a bag
there's always a Backwood
there's always a i swore i wasn't going to do this anymore
    there's always a stranger
there's always a hole
there's always redemption
there's always i got this
there's always this isn't fucking my life up bad enough to stop
there's always a nice set of wet tits
there's always a yellow bird
    there's always a yellow bird
    there's always a yellow bird
        or a blue jay
there's always Christ
there's always i love you so much it hurts when i walk
there's always summer
there's always sand in my bed
there's always intimacy issues
there's always whatever i promised when i was drunk
there's always clarity
there's always fog
there's always your bare feet on the concrete
there's always a clock
there's always a cock
there's always a yellow bird
    there's always a yellow bird
    there's always a yellow bird
        or a blue jay
but there's never eye contact

Full circle like 'O'.

EVERY AFTERNOON THE LIGHT SHINES ON THE BAR

. . . everyone all sailor blue. Drunk tongues. Stout black. Stout white. Men stocky and hard like bourbon barrels. Women with the teeth. Women that like scotch. I wore the wrong pants today. It's sunny out like drug culture. It's sunny out like a family holiday. The light quality is always better in the winter. When it comes through the window and shines on the bar. . .

Sonny,

…better if you know her middle name.

PUNDITS

We talk about
our pasts
like angry prophets
in a newsroom
debating the
ever-sought
master key of
who's-like-what and
what's-like-who
everything all venom
                      was venom
                              is venom

the lights go down
and you break character

say

the truth shall set you freedomcage

THE MERRY-GO-ROUND IN AMERICAN GODS

conditioned to mistake pinterest
summer weddings for opulence

capital T torn
capital T true

tired and hurried
like a band
being paid in vice

the worship of self
leaving us drunkenly
balanced
on a
merry-go-round

singing slow songs

        laughing carelessly

                in a mirrored globe

        this self-affirming circus

ART SHOW

I was introduced to a good poet
at an art gallery by another
artist that takes pictures of
artists doing their work
and she paints on the pictures
and glues them to larger pictures
that are then stuck to a canvas

She has many of these pieces
on the walls in the
gallery
and artists from the area come
to observe the work
and drink white wine and
eat cheese from Osco
and she gives a speech once
everyone's buzzed
and says "art is whatever
you put a frame around"
and people clap
and then go home
and talk about
subtitled movies
mostly in French

KILLER

the killer inside you is real
and the sooner you come
to terms with that
the sooner
you'll squash your potential
for killing

everybody looks the same
while being strangled

everybody is the same
once dead

unity

i've always found killers
to be honest folk
so long as they're killing

not quite like us lovers that spread it thin
far and wide
on hotel sheets
SMS code names

who am i to judge your uncle's murderer?

DON'T THINK OF AN APPLE

Remember what wind felt like in the morning
in Nepal
where people would pray like mountains
and focus the day around
feeding each other and
moving closer to an afterlife
so real you could taste it in the
fruit
        don't think of an apple.

Remember what fire felt like in a
in a hotel room
that you couldn't afford
but she was All-American and
Big Sur and dressed in red
        don't think of an apple.

Remember what it felt like
when you peeled her skin off
and she peeled your skin off
and you looked like Rothko
and she looked like an idea you had
and she felt judged
because you judged her
all Atlantic blue
and she said she would never forgive you
for those eyes
and she wanted her skin back
but you kept peeling
        don't think of an apple.

We were a God-idea
lil' Sacrificial Lamb
color me spit-roasted pig
      don't think of an apple
and a seed
and a tree
and rain
and growth
and nourishment
and roots
and who you are
and who she was to you
and who you were through her
and razorblades
and pictures of red skin
      don't think of an apple.

Remember what dirt felt like
at the place where
you could be alone to
write
and sing your songs
and fall in love
with you
with her
with you
with her
under an apple tree
under an apple tree
      you and me
           two apple seeds

Sonny,

don't live at home with me too long
because then it'll be harder for you
to build your own fire
and it wasn't until I built my own
with nothing but a matchbox and
warm fingers that I truly
saw trees for themselves

MARGOT TENENBAUM

We write a play in a Tiki bar; a comedy.

I haven't felt like this since dimensions ago.

You feel like remembering.

MISTAKING PATTERNS FOR GOD, PT. II

Rothko did a painting of a snowy
Wollaston Beach that I like. It caught
my eye some years ago on Google when
searching for the blue in everything.

It's blue and yellow and white and it reminds me
of days I would spend on the
Long Island Sound with my Uncle Bucky
catching Bluefish and Fluke.

Sometimes we'd swim to keep cool.
Hold my breath underwater,
would open my eyes and let
the salt sting
to see blue.

We'd dock feeling proud
               sun-dried dogs

Fit the human condition
               in a tackle box

Bucky'd then take me to a
restaurant with a red
or blue lighthouse to eat
clams with butter.

I once dreamt that I spoke to Rothko.
He said,
"Wollaston Beach in the winter is muted and flat."

And I said,
"The Long Island Sound in the summer is busy."
We shook hands on it.

He believed me as I believed him.

I then woke up to history's first eternal morning where
the sky looked like His paintbrush illuminating
the synesthesia in everyone,
                            the blue in everything.

That's how I fell in love with yellow.

Sonny,

protect yourself from concussions
the only birds that should be in your head
should sing like the idea of perfect
fall in love one thousand times
but remember that steel is only reliable
as long as there is no heat involved
also
don't get head in the locker room
respect yourself

MISTAKING PATTERNS FOR GOD, PT. III

When I was 19 I got beat up on Halloween by a guy dressed as the green Teletubby. I was with someone from a past life and we were drunk. I believe the altercation was over who hailed a cab first. When I was 24 I got in a car accident with a Jeep Liberty that was painted like a block of cheese; a Kraft Cruiser. Earlier that month I was visiting my mother in Connecticut and she snuck a block of Irish cheddar in my carry-on to take home. It was a small plane. Little tuna can. People were not pleased. Anyways, the driver and I got into it. We hit each other until the police arrived. Everything tasted like blood and iron for a bit and I couldn't eat cheese for a few weeks. Right before I turned 26 you moved away and I drove by our old apartment. That pizza place across the street was open. I went in and ordered a slice. There was a Mexican kid in the corner doing his Mandarin homework. The woman behind the counter said, "That's my son". I nodded and said, "Clever Kid". She smiled and gave me a slice of pepperoni. I walked outside and saw a squirrel get run over by a Jeep Liberty. It was right outside our apartment. Our old apartment where we used to live. It made me think of Teletubbies.

*WORK MYSELF TO THE BONE JUST 'CAUSE
IT'S SOMETHING TO DO*

Tidal Breathing

A mother's love's the only thing that's constant
And purpose serves what we place upon it
A thing is a thing not what you call it
Whether it's loved, hated, celebrated, demonic
And hate is an equation that is not worth solving
'Cause hate breeds a love that is ever-evolving
It shines like the sun around which we're revolving
Engaging with the come-up but the hustle is haunted
Follow your calling
Sonny, follow your calling
Your mother is calling
Your mother is calling
Sun, rain, time, light
Twenty-twenty hindsight
Sunny, Sonny, Sunny, Sonny
Put you in the limelight
Ask me what my life's like
And what it's like to die twice
Live for a millenium
Then wither like a zeitgeist
Fishnets and french women
Leave it all on the bed linen

If you peel back all my skin
You'd see I'm a real work of art

The part of me that people understand
Are reconstructed pieces of my head

You like a man with calloused hands
And good dick when you need it
And I like a girl that speaks in french
And sleeps in fishnets in the evening
I'll paint your legs long
Like Mississippi river
You can paint all my scars
Like windows with a view
Darling don't encourage this
This self-affirming circus
Everyone's a hollow shell
Searching for a purpose
I want ownership over my flaws
Stories behind all my scars
The value of a thick skin's
The value of teeth to a shark

The parts of me that people understand
Are reconstructed pieces of my head
'Cause if you saw the shit that's in my head
You'd pull a pistol, shoot me, kill me dead
Cheatin', fuckin', smokin', drinkin'
Impulse huggin' inhibition
Cold turkey sober livin
Wild turkey, all I'm thinkin'
Paint me like motherfuckin french girl

Yellow Teeth Da Di

God found me like a smoking gun
He had a gold capped tooth a silver tongue
He said all is all and one is one
What is just is, what's done is done
And then darkness crept into morning sun
And the birds sang through heaven's lungs
And I said all is all as one is one
What is just is what's done is done

Validate
Proof is truth
Who is who
Loosey goose
Boozey youth
Stupid fits
Molly pills
Big wet tits
Big ole' watch
Golden chain
Kissin' pink
Mary Jane
Know your worth
Know your lane
Know your worth
Know your lane
Make a house
Make a name
Mow your lawn
State your claim

Hold a pen
Burn a book
Fuck a verse
Jot a hook
Aimless mind
Waste some time
Give me prey
Give me life
Give me hope
Give me light
Help me cope
Help me shine
Great light shoots through me
I believe, believe
God, what sanctity
Yellow teeth, da di
Soak up all my hope
Open wide and choke
Holy, holy smoke
Choke bitch, choke bitch, choke.

Orange Sun

In the morning before anybody wake up
I be swimmin' in the liquor like a Maiko
Tryna' get a taste of this good life
Tryna' get a glimpse of the Savior
Don't you know the truth is elusive
Once you hunt for it you lose it
In the morning before anybody wake up
I be swimmin' in the liquor like a Maiko

Glued to a brand like a baby on a breast

In the morning before anybody wake up
I be swimmin' in the liquor like a Maiko
Tryna' get a taste of this good life
Tryna' slip in bed with my Saviour
Is this all there is to a fire?
Liquor and sex til I'm tired?
In the mornin' before anybody wake up
I be swimmin' in the liquor like a Maiko

Orange sun, heal me

I only consider the state of things
When I'm not trying to think
Or when I sing or drink
Clink clink clink
A blurry divide between
Day and night
Dark and light
Wrong and right

Say goodbye
Dark circles under my eyes
I'm always
Spun like the hands on a clock
Lookin' like I am what I'm not
Elegant decay
I celebrate the day
With a little bit of juice on rocks
Glued glued glued glued
To a brand like a baby on a breast
Married to a habit like a martyr to his death
We made it to the sunrise
Yes baby yes

We get up and scream so loudly
We get up and scream so proudly
The end of a Disney movie
The base of a purple drink
The face of a circle thinks
All in terms of eternal space
And I have nocturnal traits
And she is the light of day
I be where my conscience be
Bleed like an ego bleeds
Breathe like believers breathe
Die like a dog dies
Get in tune with the time of the day
That I love
When the moon gives way to the flames
Of the sun

I know
What it's like to mix faith with hot air
And I hoped
When I found my stride you'd be there
But for now
My level head sleeps gently in a flask
Or in a glass

Orange sun, heal me

Astronaut

She live her life
According to the stars
According the word
Of her people in the dive bars
Where she don't gotta try hard
Like, fuck you
And your two-step man
He live his life
According to the stars
According the pain he attain
When he lies more
He's always gotta try hard
Like how I get to be such a misfit man

And lonely lonely lonely lonely boy
Fell in love with a Twitter bot
And all the phony phony phony shit
Got her thinkin if she really wanna live or not
They both wanna be where the palm trees lean
With hearts full of fire and some soda pop
And when they sleep with their fans on medium
They're dreaming somethin big like
Oh I oughtta

I oughtta be an astronaut
'Cause empty space is all I got

And when they wake up in the morning
After dreaming of the cosmos
They abandoned all their loneliness

At bottom of a bottle
Then look for a ladder and start
From the bottom
Climb toward the sun like flowers
And heal like a problem
And when their energies collide
They fall in love like a summer month
They become the earth
And the source of its light
So they back it up
Back back to a time when
When lonely lonely lonely lonely boy
Fell in love with a Twitter bot
And all the phony phony shit
Got her thinkin if she really wanna live or not
They both wanna be where the palm trees lean
With hearts full of fire and some soda pop
And when they sleep with their fans on medium
They're dreaming something big like
Oh I oughtta

I oughtta be an astronaut
'Cause empty space is all I got
(Let their energy explode like the Fourth of July
They become the earth and the source of it's light
They fall in love like a Summer month
They become the sun and the energy inside)

Anvil

Heart heavy like an anvil, son
Heart heavy like an anvil

I mean what's a dude to do
It's just some existential dread
The queen almighty powerful
The crown upon her head
I love it when I wake up with you
Layin' in my bed
Let me love you long time
With the life that I have left
Father time takes a break
When your head is on my chest

"Samy told me time is what happens when you're dead."

A precautionary tale
Paint everything red
I mean what's a dude to do
It's just some existential dread

Gamble in a stranger's bed
My favorite way to die
I swear I'd rather be with you
You're my favorite way to die
Find me in the kitchen, cookin',
Servin' up alibis
I swear I'd rather be with you
You're my favorite way to die

Lil' Baby Elephant

I wanna wear you like a personality
So badly
Had your arms out like parallel lines
Palms up like you were channeling light
We stood tall with infinite height
Feel like kids through the night

Father time is old and gray
He's good, he's kind, he's wise, he's gay
Prepare ourselves for what he say
Like a raincoat on a sunny day
Hey say

Time don't really work like a wristwatch
And knowledge doesn't die when your lips stop
So shut your fuckin' mouth around the big dogs
But here's a bit of chiba for the lift off
Time don't really work like a wristwatch
More like parallel lines in a thick fog
Like parallel lines with your palms to the sky
Channelling light like a big dog (woof)
Time is like an evil little slut
Time is a wolf
Time is what happens when you're dead
Time is a window, keep it shut
Time is a voice in your head
Time is the beat inside your chest
I wish I could rewind time like VHS
Saint Maker, Zombie Maker, Homemaker
Be at rest 'cause

Time is like a mortgaged home
And love works like a pendulum
Love good, love hard, love true, love blind
'Cause the ones you love become your eyes

He's arrogant but affable
Pass the flask and have a pull
Love good, love hard, love true, love blind
Cause the ones you love become your eyes

Raincoat

On this highway
Thinking how she wouldn't want
To live close to a highway
Treadmill
Skyway
Only loyal to a dotted line
Atlantic gray
She used to cry like rain

Now there's little drops
of water bouncing off her raincoat
She's minute to minute
'Cause that's how the day goes
She wants to break down like sand
Where time is patient and bland

Stress weighs an ocean
Stress weighs an ocean
Confessional erosion
And all of time's motion
(Raincoat)

On these backroads
Thinking how she always wanted
To live off a back road
Treadmill
Dirt trail
Open ended like 'U'
Full circle like 'O'

Now there's little drops
Of water bouncing off her raincoat
But she don't mind 'cause she know
Her hair look good wet
She wants to break down like sand
Where time is patient and bland

No Use Cursing the Weather

No use cursing the weather
I've got nothing to prove
Work myself to the bone
Just 'cause it's something to do

It's sunny, Sonny.
Take a peek through the blinds

I'm a bonafide gorilla on my hand and my feet
And I'm just passing through this life like sand in the street
I'm like the wind in the grass
I'm like a wave at its peak
A dirty little mouth
I am a perilous freak
800-pound gorilla in a fit lookin' chic
You step under the spotlight but you can't take the heat
You freeze on first reaction, think to run, hide, and flee
But then you stand there for a lifetime so they don't think you're weak

So they don't think you're weak

I work myself to the bone just 'cause it's something to do

Head, shoulders, knees, and toes
Grab your bitch and strike a pose
Father, son, and holy spirit
Fear my fear and how I fear it
Up last night 'til a quarter past four
Just so I can say I'm no day-shift whore
Get in tune with the time of the day that I love

When the moon gives way to the flames of the sun

Anxious little waves paralyze me like ice
I got shaky Twitter fingers and a shivering spine
Waiting for the truth and my heart to align
Praying everything uncomfortable will just pass with time
I put the vodka on the ice, cut up wedges of lime
Look at these empty pill bottles it's a sign of the times
All these empty pill bottles it's a sign of the times
A little self-reflecting on the socials is fine
But the indifference of the cyberspace will swallow your strife
Look,
Whatever you prescribe to
Will someday blind you
And all those little lies you told
Will someday find you
We're all pious and righteous in our minds despite truth
Being both your best friend and a killer that knifes you
Full circle like 'O'
Open ended like 'U'
I work myself to the bone
Just 'cause it's something to do

So they don't think I'm weak

Bluefish

Lately all I do
Is stare down pixels in my living room
Begin to feel as though I'm rotting through
It burns like blisters in the afternoon
(You are pretty like a rainbow
Oil patch on a puddle)
Waiting out the winter
Standing on the doorstep
Praying for rain

You fell in love with my dark side
'Cause you love the way it shines
And I fell in love with your dark side
'Cause I love the way it shines

Was it cold outside
The place had emptied out when I arrived
I'd say otherwise
Count it lucky that we both survived
Oh doubt
Another message read too loud
Another fucked up way to begin
Oh sin
Another year will do you in
And when your heart stops
Wave me in
(You are pretty like a rainbow
oil patch on a puddle)

You are pretty like a rainbow

Plateauer

Sonny this world will teach you to
Feel like a failure 'cause you're not
One in a billion
But Sonny this world still needs you to
Peel back the layers of
Your potential brilliance

So Sonny turn your eyes
Toward any ladder you can climb
Maybe it's time to see if we can find
The blue in everything

Light up the blue in everything

Plateauer
Flatlander
Transcender
Heartbreaker
Bonecrusher
Old lovers
It's sunny outside
Take a peek through the blinds
Hey Sonny, it's sunny outside
Take a peek through the
Plateauer
Flatlander
Transcender
Heartbreaker
Warm winters
Cold summers

It's sunny outside
Take a peek through the blinds
Hey Sonny, it's sunny outside
Take a peek through the blinds
Take a peek
Tell me what you see
There's a delicacy
To this madness
Falling for the femme fatale
In the black dress
Plateauer
Flatlander
Transcender
Heartbreaker
Bonecrusher
Old lovers
Warm winters
Cold summers

Light up the blue in everything

Zombie Maker

Hold a cold rag
Back of the neck
I know why the french
Call it little death
Couple drops of blood
Bathroom tile
Checkerboard tile
Blame in my head

You're name's still on pizza box receipts

I like the way you bleed
I like the way you make me like the way I bleed
I like the way you see
I like the way you grind your teeth
Da da di

Tiny little zombie crawlin in my sleep
Talkin like it's cheap
Sayin things to me
I'm a Zombie Maker
Tripped and killed a Saint
How dare I kill a Saint
They're so hard to make

Saint Maker's in a bad dream
Galileo
Touch and go
Tadpole
Galileo

Orange sun
Summer sky
Dim light
Galileo

I'm not inspired like a man with a dead wife
Turn you into a dull ache
Useless like a rifle to a dead spy
I miss you like a dull ache
White denim with the red eyes
Strawberry stain
White paper plate
Fourth of July
Every third June
Apple for an eye
Apple of my eye
Eye for an;
Summer night holds
Different kind of moon
Different kind of mood
Mr. High-June
Summer night holds
Different kind of moon

Tiny little zombie crawlin' in my sleep
Talkin like it's cheap
Sayin things to me
I'm a Zombie Maker
Tripped and killed a Saint
How dare I kill a Saint
They're so hard to make

Balance every ounce of grace
With a drop or two of liquor
Bless it with the snowflake
And then hit it with the mixer
Zombie Maker Zombie Maker
Got my finger on the trigger
A lover is a lover
As a killer is a killer
Hot and cold like Christmas Eve
Was deep in the summer
Breathe and I wonder
What kind of Uncle I'd see in my brother
Get it together and put it back
Piece by piece with my lover
And be the hunter that they need
While never feedin' my hunger
The orange sun shines in the evening bright
And a sunflower never turns on what feeds it light
But Jesus Christ I'm a heathen
A fiend in the night
And fear awakens the beast and the demons inside
I'm afraid you'll see me
And reveal the disguise
Swallow a heart whole baby
Conceal the device
The orgasm from hell
But the feeling was nice
It's easy to see you're
The only reason I write

She said
"Samy is it only real
To you if you can hold it?
Why you choose to see this
As a burden to cope with?
Don't you think it's beautiful
And worthy of focus?"
I said,
"I'm tongue-tied as fuck
They should've sent a poet"

Rothko

It's sunny, Sonny.

Swallow a dollar &
Shit out a bitcoin
Cyberspace
Cyberwaste
I really am a big boy
Loss of self in nation
In this nation, I'm created
America the
Holy shit look at that
Fuckin facelift
Put money on the table
Cook a song up in the oven
Does the Benzo got the wood grain baby
Tell me who you fuckin'
Loss of self in nation
In this nation I am cloaked in
Keep your dildo in your safe
And your handgun in your holster
Sex is better when you know her
If you know her middle name
A bit of sexy devastation
In a perfect little frame
If you fall in love a thousand times
And each time feels the same
Put your heart on top a shelf
And trust it shall remain
But if you find a yellow bird
That flies as high as planes

And sings a song of summer
You should muster up and say
"From anxiety to timeless sleep
I've missed you like rain
Rattle me like thunder
And then wash away the pain"

I never bothered with brick and mortar
Only ever bothered with the matters of the heart
Find the inner outside
Inner outside of your mind
Find a means to an end that leads to a start

America the beautiful
Got blue blood in my veins
Scratching at my jugular
While thinkin' somethin' strange
Don't act so surprised
When people don't make a change
Or when they do but
Pretend to be the same
Saint Maker Saint Maker
Make me a Saint
Give me a name
And a soul I can save
Angel-faced God fearing
Mother-lovin' beauties
No fear of losing
What they got worth losing
Then it's click click click
On to the new thing
Silicon ass cheeks

Rachel McAdams eating poutine
I like what I think
You could use some fine tuning
Abusing a telephone
You didn't know you were abusing
This is me eating steak
This is me going vegan
This is me being single
This is me in cuffing season
This is me doing good
This is me doing well
This is me signing off
To deal with my personal hell

This world will have you feel like a failure
Because you're not one in a billion
That you'll work your whole life
Only to be almost brilliant
But all the wear and tear
Will make your skin resilient
And in the end you'll be made of
Scarred flesh and fulfillment

www.ingramcontent.com/pod-product-compliance
Lightning Source LLC
Chambersburg PA
CBHW042253100526
44587CB00003B/122